Retirement's Resourceful Riches

Securing retirement wealth through responsible financial planning, minimizing tax liability during retirement

Xavier Hartfield

Table of Contents

1 Chapter 1: Planning Your Retirement

Defining your financial goals is the cornerstone of successful retirement planning. Think deeply about your desired lifestyle: Do you envision leisurely travels, pursuing hobbies, or contributing to your community? Quantify these aspirations. How much will your dream vacation cost annually? What are the ongoing expenses of your passions? Detailed budgeting, going beyond simple needs, is critical; include projected healthcare, entertainment, and potential unexpected costs. This comprehensive picture helps you determine the required nest egg. Ignoring this crucial step is like charting a course without a destination; you'll likely find yourself adrift without a clear understanding of what you're aiming for. The more specific you are, the better you can make informed financial decisions now to achieve your goals. This isn't simply about numbers; it's about crafting a vision of your ideal retirement and building a financial plan that makes it a reality. Remember to adjust your goals as needed; life's changes may necessitate a reevaluation. It's not set in stone.

Creating a realistic retirement timeline is equally vital. Consider your current age, planned retirement age, and your anticipated lifespan. Factor in any expected changes in income, like potential salary increases or anticipated job transitions. Consult actuarial tables for life expectancy data tailored to your demographic. These numbers create a framework for your saving strategy. Are you on track to accumulate the necessary funds? If not, this timeline allows you to adjust your saving strategy accordingly; possibly increase contributions, explore additional investment options, or postpone retirement slightly. Furthermore, factor in potential life events, like unexpected medical expenses or family emergencies. Having a buffer in place can make unexpected circumstances more manageable. The timeline is not simply a countdown; it's a dynamic tool that guides your financial actions, allowing you to adjust your course as needed. It's about continuous monitoring and proactive adjustments.

The process of projecting future expenses and income streams requires careful consideration of several factors. Analyze your current spending habits, identifying both essential and discretionary expenses. Project how these expenses might change in retirement. You'll likely have less expenditure on work-related costs, but increased expenses from leisure pursuits and healthcare. Consider inflation's impact on the cost of goods and services; your expenses in 20 years will significantly differ from those today. For income, factor in your anticipated retirement savings, pensions, Social Security benefits, and any potential part-time income. It's helpful to seek professional advice from a financial planner; they can offer sophisticated projections, accounting for various scenarios, and help you to refine your estimations. Remember, the more precise your projections, the more effective your retirement plan can be. Accurately estimating your future financial needs and income is crucial to securing a financially comfortable retirement. A realistic approach, rather than optimism, will lead to more reliable outcomes.

Building a robust retirement plan is not a solitary endeavor. Seek professional advice from a financial advisor who can provide personalized guidance. Explain your financial goals, risk tolerance, and timeline. A financial advisor, with their expertise, can help you choose appropriate investment strategies and retirement vehicles that align with your situation. Don't hesitate to seek multiple opinions; compare advice and strategies from different professionals. Their recommendations should be tailored to your specific circumstances, considering your individual financial profile, risk tolerance, and long-term goals. This professional collaboration ensures that your plan is built upon a solid foundation of financial knowledge and expertise, providing better outcomes compared to a self-directed approach. Remember, retirement planning is complex; professional guidance streamlines the process and maximizes your chances of success. Their knowledge helps avoid costly mistakes, reducing stress and uncertainties during this crucial life stage.

1.1 Financial Goals

Defining your financial goals is the cornerstone of a secure retirement. It's not just about a number; it's about envisioning your ideal retirement lifestyle and translating that vision into concrete, measurable objectives. Do you dream of traveling extensively? Perhaps owning a vacation home is part of your plan? Or maybe you simply envision relaxing days filled with hobbies and spending time with loved ones, free from the pressures of daily work. Each of these desires has a financial cost, and understanding those costs is the first critical step. Consider your current lifestyle. What are your essential monthly expenses? Housing, transportation, food, utilities—these are the bedrock of your spending. Now, project those expenses into retirement, accounting for inflation. Healthcare costs, often overlooked, will likely increase significantly. Plan for this realistically. Don't underestimate your healthcare expenses. Unexpected medical bills can severely impact your retirement finances if not planned for in advance.

Next, examine your income sources. Will you rely solely on retirement savings and Social Security? Do you anticipate receiving a pension? Will you need part-time work to supplement your income? These are vital questions to honestly address. A clear picture of your potential income streams is necessary to accurately assess the financial gap you need to bridge before retirement. It's about creating a realistic financial profile, both current and projected.

Now comes the crucial part—bridging that gap between your projected expenses and income. This will determine the size of your retirement nest egg. This requires careful calculation and may involve adjustments to your lifestyle aspirations or a more aggressive approach to saving and investing. Consider seeking professional financial advice; a qualified advisor can help analyze your situation and develop a personalized plan that maximizes your chances of success.

This isn't about deprivation; it's about intelligent planning. You may need to adjust your timeline. Perhaps you need to work a few more years to reach your financial goals. Or you might need to reduce some non-essential expenses along the way. This doesn't mean sacrificing happiness; it means making informed choices that align with your long-term financial well-being.

Moreover, regular review is essential. Your financial situation is dynamic. Unexpected events—job loss, medical emergencies—can disrupt even the most carefully crafted plan. Regularly reviewing and adjusting your goals and investment strategy ensures you stay on track. This flexibility is essential for navigating the unexpected curveballs life throws your way. Don't consider your retirement plan static; treat it as an evolving document reflecting your current reality.

Beyond the numbers, consider your non-financial goals. Retirement isn't solely about money; it's about achieving personal fulfillment. Consider the activities you enjoy and how you envision spending your time. This contributes to a holistic view of your retirement, ensuring it's not just financially secure but also personally enriching. Integrate those lifestyle considerations into your financial planning.

Financial goals aren't simply about accumulating wealth; they are about security and peace of mind. It's about knowing you have the resources to live comfortably, pursue your passions, and enjoy the next chapter of your life without undue financial stress. By setting clear, realistic financial goals and diligently pursuing them, you pave the way for a successful and fulfilling retirement. Remember, proactive planning is the key to unlocking financial freedom in your golden years. Start planning early; the sooner you begin, the more time you have to reach your objectives. Don't delay; your future self will thank you. This is not just about money; it's about securing your future and your peace of mind. Begin with a clear vision of your ideal retirement, and let that vision guide your every financial decision.

1.2 Retirement Timeline

A realistic retirement timeline isn't a single, rigid number; it's a dynamic process. Begin by honestly assessing your current financial situation. This includes tallying assets like savings, investments, and property, as well as debts such as mortgages, loans, and credit card balances. Understanding your net worth provides a foundational benchmark. Don't underestimate the power of detailed record-keeping; meticulous tracking offers clarity and allows for informed decisions.

Next, project your future income. This goes beyond just your anticipated pension or Social Security benefits. Consider potential part-time work, rental income, or any other supplemental income streams. Remember to account for potential fluctuations in income based on market conditions or health considerations. Be conservative in your estimations; it's better to slightly underestimate than overestimate potential income.

Simultaneously, estimate your future expenses. This requires careful consideration of your desired lifestyle in retirement. Factor in everyday essentials such as housing, groceries, utilities, and transportation, but also include leisure activities, travel, and healthcare costs. Research average retirement costs in your area to build a more accurate picture. Consider inflation too; projecting expenses without adjusting for inflation can lead to significant underestimation. Thorough planning is essential.

Now, we can begin to visualize your retirement timeline. This isn't about picking a specific age; it's about aligning your projected income and expenses with your savings goals. If you aim for retirement at a specific age, work backward from that date. Analyze how your current savings and projected income will suffice to cover your estimated expenses for that period. This analysis could reveal a necessary adjustment in your savings habits or a need to postpone retirement.

If the analysis reveals a shortfall, don't panic. There are various strategies you can implement. You might consider working longer, which would allow you to increase your savings or reduce the retirement period needing funding. Alternatively, you could explore reducing your anticipated expenses through adjustments in your planned lifestyle. Every individual's situation is unique, prompting the need for personalized adjustments and proactive planning.

Remember, this is an iterative process. Regularly review and update your timeline. Life throws curveballs; unexpected events such as health issues or market downturns can significantly impact your financial outlook. Annual (or even semi-annual) reviews are recommended. Adjustments to your timeline might involve reducing spending, seeking additional income, or re-evaluating your investment strategy. Flexibility is key.

Furthermore, consult with a financial advisor. They can offer invaluable professional guidance. A financial planner can help you navigate the complexities of retirement planning, offering personalized strategies for reaching your financial goals. They'll provide objective insights you may not have considered, further refining your approach to achieving a secure and comfortable retirement. Don't hesitate to seek professional assistance; it's a valuable investment in your future.

Finally, remember that your retirement timeline is a personalized roadmap. It's not about achieving a pre-defined, arbitrary age, but securing financial stability and well-being for the years ahead. It's a journey that requires consistent effort and adjustment based on changing circumstances. By proactively monitoring your financial health, regularly reviewing your timeline, and seeking professional guidance where necessary, you can confidently navigate the path towards a secure and fulfilling retirement. The process itself is part of the journey; embrace the learning and adaptation involved, and remember the ultimate goal: a retirement you can truly enjoy. Your planning today secures your tomorrow. Don't just react; prepare. Don't just dream; build.

2 Chapter 2: Investment Strategies

Diversification is paramount. Don't put all your eggs in one basket, as the old adage wisely advises. Spread your investments across various asset classes–stocks, bonds, real estate, even alternative investments like commodities–to reduce the impact of any single market downturn. A well-diversified portfolio is more resilient to market fluctuations, offering a smoother ride towards your retirement goal. This isn't about getting rich quick; it's about building a stable, long-term foundation. Consider your risk tolerance carefully; aggressive investors might favor a higher stock allocation, while more conservative individuals might lean towards bonds and fixed-income securities. Remember, your risk tolerance may change over time, so regular portfolio reviews are essential. Professional financial advice can significantly aid in constructing a suitable diversified portfolio tailored to your specific needs and circumstances.

Understanding your risk tolerance is crucial before making any investment decisions. Are you comfortable with potential short-term losses in pursuit of higher long-term gains? Or do you prioritize capital preservation above all else? Consider your emotional response to market volatility. A questionnaire might help you quantify this, or even a frank discussion with a financial advisor. A common mistake beginners make is chasing high returns without fully understanding the associated risks. A properly assessed risk tolerance will guide your investment choices, helping you avoid impulsive decisions driven by fear or greed. Remember, consistent returns, even if modest, are far more valuable in the long run than erratic, high-risk ventures. Invest within your comfort zone to ensure you remain invested throughout the journey to retirement. Remember that investing is a long-term game, and patience is a key virtue.

Long-term growth is the core objective of any successful retirement investment strategy. We're not talking about quick schemes or get-rich-quick plans; this is about consistently building wealth over decades. This requires patience, discipline, and a focus on sustainable, long-term returns. Investing in index funds or exchange-traded funds (ETFs) that track broad market indices can provide diversified exposure to a wide range of companies and sectors. Consider dollar-cost averaging, a strategy that involves investing a fixed amount of money at regular intervals, regardless of market fluctuations. This helps to mitigate the risk of investing a lump sum at a market peak. Furthermore, regular contributions, even small ones, compounded over time, can yield significant returns. Reinvest your dividends and capital gains to accelerate the growth of your portfolio. Remember the power of compounding; it is the cornerstone of long-term wealth building. This means letting your earnings generate more earnings over time, and it's a very powerful tool when you want to achieve your long-term goals. Consistent, disciplined investing, even in a bear market, creates a much higher return over time.

The power of compounding isn't merely theoretical; it's a proven principle of finance. Imagine starting with a relatively modest investment and consistently reinvesting your earnings over 30 or 40 years. The accumulated returns can be astonishing, far exceeding what you might initially expect. This illustrates the importance of starting early and maintaining a consistent investment strategy. Early contributions benefit greatly from the extended period of compounding. The longer your money is invested, the more significant the impact of this compounding effect will be. This principle is fundamental to securing your financial future and building sufficient wealth for a comfortable retirement. Your initial investment, while important, takes second place to the power of compounding over time. It allows you to reach your retirement goal sooner than you expect.

Tax-advantaged retirement accounts can significantly enhance your long-term returns. These accounts, like 401(k)s and IRAs, offer tax benefits that boost your savings. Understanding the rules and regulations of different account types is vital for maximizing your tax advantages. For instance, contributions to traditional 401(k)s are tax-deductible, reducing your current taxable income. However, withdrawals in retirement are taxed as ordinary income. Roth accounts offer tax-free withdrawals in retirement, although contributions aren't tax-deductible. Careful consideration of your current tax bracket and projected retirement income is key to selecting the most beneficial type of account. Seek professional advice when weighing your tax options and choosing the right accounts. The complexities of tax laws can be difficult to navigate alone, and professional advice is highly recommended. It will avoid costly mistakes in the future and help you achieve a better investment strategy.

Remember, this is a marathon, not a sprint. Building long-term wealth requires patience, discipline, and a long-term perspective. Don't let short-term market fluctuations deter you from your retirement goals. Stay focused on your long-term strategy, and periodically review and adjust your plan as needed. Regular reviews aren't just about reacting to market changes; they're also about ensuring your investment strategy continues to align with your evolving financial goals and personal circumstances. Your goals and circumstances will change as you age; make sure your investment strategy adapts to the changes. It might involve increasing the risk level while you're younger and reducing risk when approaching retirement. This long-term approach will help achieve the best possible results.

2.1 Diversification Tactics

Diversification isn't just a buzzword; it's the cornerstone of a robust retirement investment strategy. Think of it as spreading your financial eggs across multiple baskets, reducing the impact of any single basket breaking. This isn't about simply owning different stocks; it's a nuanced approach encompassing diverse asset classes, minimizing risk, and maximizing your chances of achieving long-term growth. A well-diversified portfolio isn't static; it requires regular review and adjustments based on market conditions and your evolving financial goals.

Asset allocation is the heart of diversification. This involves strategically distributing your investment funds across various asset classes, each possessing unique risk and return profiles. These classes generally include stocks (equities), bonds (fixed income), real estate, and alternative investments like commodities or private equity. The optimal allocation depends heavily on your risk tolerance, time horizon until retirement, and your specific financial goals. A younger investor with a longer time horizon might comfortably allocate a larger percentage to stocks, accepting higher risk for potentially greater returns. Conversely, someone nearing retirement might favor a more conservative approach, shifting towards bonds to preserve capital.

Understanding your risk tolerance is paramount. This isn't merely about your comfort level with potential losses; it's a careful evaluation of your entire financial situation and personal circumstances. Factors such as your income security, emergency fund, and debt levels heavily influence your ability to withstand market downturns. Honest self-assessment is crucial; a financial advisor can assist in this process, providing valuable insights and objective perspectives. Remember, while higher risk can lead to higher potential rewards, it also increases the possibility of substantial losses.

Stocks, representing ownership in companies, are traditionally considered the highest-risk, highest-reward asset class. However, within the stock market itself lies further diversification opportunities. Consider investing in different sectors (technology, healthcare, energy), market capitalization (large-cap, mid-cap, small-cap), and geographical regions (domestic, international, emerging markets). This approach reduces the impact of any single sector or market underperforming. Bonds, on the other hand, generally offer lower returns but provide greater stability, acting as a buffer during market volatility. Diversifying within the bond market can involve different maturities (short-term, long-term), credit ratings (investment grade, high-yield), and issuers (government, corporate, municipal).

Real estate can serve as another valuable diversification tool. Owning a rental property can generate passive income, while appreciating property values contribute to long-term growth. However, real estate investments are illiquid, meaning they can be difficult to sell quickly. This should be considered carefully alongside your overall financial plan. Alternative investments such as commodities (gold, oil) or private equity offer unique characteristics; commodities can act as inflation hedges, while private equity provides access to potentially high-growth businesses, but both typically involve higher risks and liquidity constraints.

Regular portfolio rebalancing is essential for maintaining your desired asset allocation. Market fluctuations will inevitably cause your portfolio to drift from its target allocation over time. Rebalancing involves selling some assets that have performed well and buying others that have underperformed to return the portfolio to its original allocation. This disciplined approach helps to prevent excessive risk concentration and capitalize on market movements. The frequency of rebalancing depends on individual circumstances and investment goals; some investors might rebalance annually, while others might do it quarterly or even semi-annually.

Finally, remember that diversification isn't a guaranteed path to riches; it's a risk-mitigation strategy aimed at maximizing your chances of achieving your retirement goals. No investment strategy is entirely without risk, and market conditions can always be unpredictable. However, through careful planning, diversification, and regular monitoring, you can significantly enhance your prospects for a secure and comfortable retirement. This holistic approach, combined with sound financial planning, allows you to build wealth and reduce your potential for financial losses, thereby securing your future. It's a continuous process of review and adjustment, one that will ultimately pay significant dividends.

2.2 Risk Tolerance Assessment

Understanding your risk tolerance is paramount to successful retirement planning. It dictates the types of investments suitable for your portfolio and significantly influences your overall financial strategy. Ignoring this crucial element can lead to unnecessary stress and potential losses, jeopardizing your retirement security. A well-defined risk tolerance profile isn't just about numbers; it's about understanding your emotional response to market fluctuations and aligning your investment strategy with your comfort level.

Before diving into specific questionnaires, let's clarify what risk tolerance actually means. It's not simply about how much money you can afford to lose; it's a multifaceted assessment encompassing your emotional resilience, financial situation, and time horizon. Someone with a high net worth and a long time until retirement might tolerate greater risk than someone nearing retirement with limited savings. This isn't about bravery or recklessness; it's about making informed choices that align with your individual circumstances.

Several methods exist to determine your risk tolerance. The most common approach involves completing a questionnaire, often found online or provided by financial advisors. These questionnaires typically assess your investment experience, financial knowledge, comfort level with potential losses, and your overall financial goals. However, relying solely on a questionnaire can be insufficient. A more holistic approach combines self-assessment with a comprehensive discussion with a qualified financial advisor. They can help you interpret your results within the context of your broader financial picture.

Consider your time horizon. Younger investors generally have a longer time to recover from potential market downturns, allowing them to embrace higher-risk investments with potentially greater rewards. Conversely, those closer to retirement often prioritize capital preservation, opting for lower-risk investments to safeguard their retirement savings. This timeframe significantly impacts your investment choices. Remember, investment strategies should adapt to your life stage, so regular review is vital.

Your personal circumstances significantly shape your risk tolerance. Factors such as existing debt, emergency savings, and other sources of income all contribute to your overall financial resilience. If you have substantial debt or limited emergency funds, a more conservative approach might be necessary. Conversely, a robust emergency fund and minimal debt can provide a buffer, allowing you to absorb potential investment losses more readily.

Beyond the quantitative aspects, your emotional response to market volatility plays a critical role. Some investors are comfortable with the ups and downs of the market, while others find it incredibly stressful. Your emotional reaction significantly influences your decision-making ability during periods of market uncertainty. Honest self-reflection on how you react to financial news is crucial for determining your true risk tolerance. Don't underestimate the power of your emotions on your investment decisions.

Once you've assessed your risk tolerance, it's crucial to translate this understanding into a concrete investment strategy. This involves selecting asset classes (stocks, bonds, real estate, etc.) that align with your risk profile. A higher risk tolerance might justify a larger allocation to stocks, offering potentially higher returns but also increased volatility. Conversely, a lower risk tolerance might dictate a more conservative approach, with a greater emphasis on bonds and other fixed-income securities. It's a continuous process of balancing risk and return.

Regularly reviewing and adjusting your risk tolerance is crucial. Life circumstances change, and what feels comfortable at one point might feel different later. Significant life events, changes in your financial situation, or even shifts in your emotional state can affect your risk tolerance. Schedule a review with your financial advisor at least annually to ensure your investment strategy continues to align with your current risk profile and retirement goals. This consistent monitoring is key to managing your investments effectively throughout your retirement planning.

Remember, determining your risk tolerance is a personal journey. There is no one-size-fits-all answer. By carefully considering your financial situation, time horizon, emotional response to risk, and seeking professional guidance, you can develop a sound investment strategy tailored to your specific needs and goals. This process ensures a more confident and secure retirement journey. Embrace the process, seek professional guidance, and make informed decisions based on a realistic assessment of your risk tolerance. Your future self will thank you.

2.3 Long-Term Growth

Index funds, offering broad market exposure at low costs, represent a cornerstone of long-term growth strategies. Their diversification inherently mitigates risk, a crucial factor when aiming for consistent returns over decades. Consider allocating a significant portion of your retirement portfolio to index funds, harnessing the power of compounding returns without the need for constant market timing or active management. This passive approach minimizes fees and emotional decision-making, both of which can significantly impact your long-term success. Remember that consistency and patience are key; avoid reacting to short-term market fluctuations.

Real estate investment trusts (REITs) provide another avenue for diversification and potential long-term gains. REITs offer exposure to the real estate market without the complexities of direct property ownership. Their dividends often offer a higher yield compared to other investments, contributing to consistent income generation during retirement. However, it's important to carefully analyze the specific REITs, understanding their underlying assets and management strategies before investing. Diversifying your REIT holdings across different property types and geographical locations can help reduce individual risk.

Growth stocks, characterized by high potential for appreciation, deserve consideration within a diversified portfolio. However, it's essential to balance growth stocks with more conservative investments. Their inherent volatility requires careful consideration of your risk tolerance. Thorough research and due diligence are paramount; focusing on companies with strong fundamentals, sustainable competitive advantages, and consistent revenue growth is key. Don't chase short-term market trends, instead focusing on companies with a proven track record and a clear vision for the future.

Bonds, while offering lower returns than stocks, act as a crucial ballast within a retirement portfolio, reducing overall volatility. Consider investing in a mix of government and corporate bonds to spread risk. Their predictable income stream provides a level of stability crucial during retirement, when consistent cash flow is critical. Furthermore, bonds tend to perform inversely to stocks, offering a buffer during market downturns. This balance reduces portfolio fluctuations, which is crucial for long-term security. Regularly rebalancing your portfolio, adjusting bond and stock allocations to maintain your desired risk level, will be a cornerstone of your strategy.

Don't neglect the importance of regular portfolio rebalancing. Market fluctuations will inevitably cause the proportions of your assets to shift over time. Rebalancing involves selling some of your assets that have performed well and buying more of those that have underperformed, bringing your portfolio back to your target asset allocation. This disciplined approach helps to control risk and maintain a balance between risk and reward aligned with your long-term goals. It's not about timing the market but about maintaining your desired exposure to different asset classes.

While the allure of high-yield investments might be tempting, the importance of assessing your personal risk tolerance cannot be overstated. It's a critical step in developing a long-term investment strategy tailored to your specific needs and circumstances. Understanding your comfort level with potential losses is essential in choosing appropriate investment vehicles, and helps prevent rash decisions during periods of market volatility. Your risk tolerance should inform not just your investment selection but also your overall financial plan, ensuring that your retirement goals are realistically achievable.

Retirement planning involves a long-term perspective; short-term market fluctuations should not dictate your investment decisions. Consistent contributions to your retirement accounts are paramount, even during periods of economic uncertainty. The power of compounding returns is a fundamental principle of successful long-term investing, and consistently contributing, regardless of market conditions, will help you reach your retirement goals. Discipline and patience are virtues often tested but crucial in securing your long-term financial security.

Remember that professional financial advice can be invaluable. A certified financial planner can help you create a personalized retirement plan, providing tailored guidance based on your individual circumstances, risk tolerance, and financial objectives. They can assess your current financial situation and provide guidance on asset allocation, risk management, and tax optimization strategies, ensuring your plan aligns with your specific goals. This partnership can provide an essential support system for the journey to retirement.

Finally, staying informed about your investments and the broader economic climate is vital for successful long-term growth. Regularly review your investment portfolio, paying attention to performance and adjusting your strategy as needed. Remaining informed will allow you to react intelligently to changing economic conditions, making informed decisions that support your long-term goals. While you shouldn't overreact to every market shift, consistent monitoring and informed adjustments will support your success. Your retirement's financial health is a marathon, not a sprint, demanding perseverance, consistency, and sound planning.

3 Chapter 3: Retirement Accounts

Understanding and leveraging retirement accounts is paramount to securing your financial future. Choosing the right account depends heavily on your individual circumstances, including your income, risk tolerance, and long-term financial goals. It's not a one-size-fits-all solution; careful consideration is key.

Traditional Individual Retirement Accounts (IRAs) and 401(k) plans offer significant tax advantages during your working years. Contributions are often tax-deductible, reducing your current taxable income. However, withdrawals in retirement are taxed as ordinary income. This means you'll pay taxes on the money you withdraw, potentially impacting your overall retirement income. It's crucial to factor this into your overall retirement planning. Carefully consider your current tax bracket and your projected tax bracket in retirement when making decisions about contributions to these accounts.

Roth IRAs offer a different approach. Contributions aren't tax-deductible, meaning you pay taxes upfront. The advantage lies in tax-free withdrawals in retirement. This makes Roth IRAs particularly attractive for those who anticipate being in a higher tax bracket during retirement than they are currently. They offer a considerable benefit for long-term tax savings, but remember, you're paying taxes now for tax-free benefits later. The timing of your contributions, therefore, is crucial for maximizing this advantage. Weighing the immediate tax implications against the long-term tax benefits requires careful consideration of your personal financial situation and projections for the future. Seek professional advice if you are unsure which option best suits your needs.

Pensions and annuities provide a more structured income stream during retirement. Pensions, typically offered through employers, offer a guaranteed monthly payment, providing a sense of financial security. Annuities, purchased individually, are contracts that provide a stream of payments, often with options for guaranteed income or growth potential. Understanding the different types of annuities and the associated fees is crucial before committing. It is important to understand the various features and fees of annuities, such as surrender charges and expense ratios. Compare these aspects with the income projections to make informed decisions. Be wary of high fees that could drastically erode your retirement savings.

Roth conversions allow you to move funds from a traditional IRA or 401(k) to a Roth IRA. While this involves paying taxes on the converted amount now, it offers the benefit of tax-free withdrawals in retirement. The strategy is most beneficial for those who anticipate being in a higher tax bracket in retirement. However, careful consideration is necessary; it may not be the best move for everyone, and the timing of such conversions should be strategically planned. Consider your income and anticipated tax brackets, both now and in the future; professional financial advice can be invaluable in making this decision, as there are potential tax penalties associated with premature withdrawals.

Beyond IRAs and 401(k)s, explore other tax-advantaged accounts. Health Savings Accounts (HSAs), for example, offer a triple tax advantage: contributions are tax-deductible, earnings grow tax-deferred, and withdrawals for qualified medical expenses are tax-free. This is especially valuable given rising healthcare costs in retirement. These accounts can serve as a valuable tool for managing healthcare expenses, offering flexibility in retirement and reducing your overall tax liability. Their utility is primarily linked to your health care needs and the level of your medical expenses.

Effective account management is essential for maximizing your retirement savings. This involves regularly reviewing your investments, ensuring they align with your risk tolerance and long-term goals. Diversification is also critical, spreading your investments across different asset classes to minimize risk. Rebalancing your portfolio periodically to maintain your desired asset allocation is also highly recommended. This ensures your portfolio remains aligned with your risk tolerance and investment objectives. Regularly monitoring your accounts for fees and expenses is also a key aspect of effective account management. Understanding these fees and expenses is crucial to understand their impact on your investment returns.

The specifics of your retirement account strategy should reflect your unique situation. This chapter provides only a general overview. Consulting with a qualified financial advisor is strongly recommended to develop a personalized retirement plan tailored to your individual financial circumstances, risk tolerance, and long-term goals. Remember, your retirement security is a significant goal. By carefully managing your retirement accounts and making informed choices, you significantly improve your chances of achieving a financially secure and fulfilling retirement.

3.1 IRAs & 401(k)s

Traditional IRAs offer a tax-deferred growth advantage. Contributions may be tax-deductible, depending on your income and whether you or your spouse is covered by a retirement plan at work. The earnings grow tax-free until withdrawal in retirement, at which point you'll pay income tax on the distributions. Consider the tax implications carefully, especially if you anticipate being in a higher tax bracket during retirement than you are currently. Remember, this is a long-term investment; your patience will be rewarded.

401(k) plans, on the other hand, are employer-sponsored retirement savings plans. Many employers offer matching contributions, essentially providing free money towards your retirement. This is a significant benefit you shouldn't ignore. However, understand the vesting schedule; this defines how long you must work for the company to fully own the employer's matching contributions. Before transferring your 401(k) after leaving a job, explore all your options – leaving it with your previous employer might be the most cost-effective choice.

The contribution limits for both IRAs and 401(k)s are adjusted annually to account for inflation; therefore, you should always consult the IRS website for the most up-to-date figures. Understanding these limits is crucial for maximizing your tax advantages and retirement savings. Stay informed; knowledge is power when it comes to personal finance. Don't be afraid to seek professional advice; a financial advisor can help you navigate the complexities of retirement planning and optimize your contributions.

Roth IRAs provide a different approach. Contributions aren't tax-deductible, but withdrawals in retirement are tax-free. This strategy proves beneficial if you expect to be in a higher tax bracket during retirement. Weigh the immediate tax implications against the long-term tax benefits carefully. This choice depends greatly on individual circumstances and projected future tax rates, making thoughtful planning essential. A financial advisor can assist in determining the best strategy for your specific situation.

Roth 401(k)s combine elements of both traditional and Roth IRAs. Contributions are made with after-tax dollars, but withdrawals during retirement are tax-free. These plans offer the same tax advantages as Roth IRAs but may have higher contribution limits. Understanding the differences between traditional and Roth accounts is vital for making informed decisions about where to allocate your retirement savings. Consider your current and anticipated future tax situations when making this critical decision.

Diversification within your retirement accounts is just as important as the type of account you choose. Don't put all your eggs in one basket. Consider diversifying your investments across different asset classes, such as stocks, bonds, and real estate, to minimize risk. Rebalance your portfolio periodically to maintain your desired asset allocation.

This prevents undue concentration in specific asset classes and mitigates potential losses stemming from market volatility. Regular review and adjustment are paramount for long-term success.

Accessing your retirement savings before retirement typically involves penalties. Withdrawals from traditional IRAs and 401(k)s are subject to both income tax and a 10% early withdrawal penalty if taken before age 59 1/2. There are certain exceptions, such as for first-time home purchases or significant medical expenses, but it's usually best to avoid early withdrawals if possible. Planning for retirement starts today, not when you're already in your golden years; it's a matter of planning and disciplined saving.

Remember that this information is for general guidance only; consult with a qualified financial advisor or tax professional for personalized advice tailored to your specific financial situation. They can help you navigate the complexities of retirement planning and develop a strategy that aligns with your goals and risk tolerance. Don't underestimate the value of professional guidance; having an expert by your side offers peace of mind and significantly enhances your chances of success. Your future self will thank you for the proactive approach you took today. Retirement planning is a journey, not a destination, and professional guidance assists in making your journey smoother and more effective. Take advantage of the resources available to make informed decisions and secure a comfortable future for yourself.

3.2 Pensions & Annuities

Defined contribution plans, like 401(k)s, offer a degree of control and portability absent in traditional pensions. However, the responsibility for investment success rests squarely on the individual. Careful planning and diversification are key to maximizing returns and mitigating risks. Remember to regularly review your portfolio's performance and adjust your strategy as needed, adapting to market fluctuations and your evolving financial goals. Seeking advice from a qualified financial advisor can be invaluable, particularly when navigating complex investment options or considering the long-term implications of different investment strategies. Understanding the fee structures associated with various investment options is crucial; seemingly small percentages can significantly impact your overall returns over time, especially during the crucial decades before retirement. Don't underestimate the power of compounding returns, especially when starting earlier.

Unlike defined contribution plans, traditional pensions guarantee a regular income stream during retirement, often providing a sense of financial security. This guaranteed income can be especially helpful in budgeting and planning for essential expenses. However, the downside lies in their limited flexibility and often stricter withdrawal rules. Additionally, the financial health of the pension plan itself plays a critical role, influencing the longevity and stability of your benefits. Understanding the specific rules and regulations governing your pension plan is therefore crucial. The vesting period, which dictates how long you must contribute before benefits are fully guaranteed, should be a key factor in your long-term financial planning, determining your investment strategies and overall retirement preparedness. Furthermore, it is prudent to familiarize yourself with the benefits calculation methodology used by your pension plan. This will assist in projecting your future retirement income accurately.

Annuities, on the other hand, are financial products that offer a steady stream of income for a specified period, typically throughout retirement. They provide a form of guaranteed income, similar to pensions, but with more flexibility in terms of how the payments are structured. Immediate annuities start paying out immediately, providing a dependable source of income from the day of purchase. Deferred annuities, conversely, allow you to postpone income payments to a later date, often enabling you to benefit from tax-deferred growth in the interim. The choice between an immediate or deferred annuity will depend largely on your individual financial circumstances, risk tolerance, and specific retirement goals. Consider your timeline for retirement income and your overall risk profile when making this decision.

Several types of annuities exist, each with its own set of characteristics and benefits. Fixed annuities provide a guaranteed rate of return, offering predictable income streams. Variable annuities, conversely, invest in a variety of market sectors, potentially offering higher returns but also exposing you to higher risks. Indexed annuities seek to balance growth potential with a degree of protection against market downturns. Before selecting any annuity, meticulously analyze the fees associated with each. Hidden fees can significantly erode returns, negating the benefits of the product itself. Thoroughly research and compare different annuity options from multiple reputable providers, ensuring a clear understanding of all terms and conditions before committing your funds.

The tax implications of pensions and annuities are significant and can influence your overall retirement income strategy. Understanding how these products are taxed throughout your retirement is crucial for effective financial planning. Many pension plans are tax-deferred, meaning you defer tax payments until you begin receiving distributions. These distributions are often taxed at your ordinary income tax rate during retirement. Conversely, annuity payments may be subject to both income tax and additional taxes depending on factors like the type of annuity and how it was funded. Tax-efficient retirement planning requires a careful evaluation of how these products interact with your overall tax liability, and it's advisable to seek guidance from a tax professional. Proper tax planning can often significantly enhance your overall retirement income and reduce your tax burden during the golden years.

Considering the longevity of retirement, a well-structured plan that combines different approaches is usually the most secure and adaptable. A diversified strategy incorporating a defined contribution plan, a traditional pension if available, and possibly a supplemental annuity can provide a more robust and resilient income stream. It's crucial to remain flexible and adapt your strategy as your circumstances change; this is particularly important during the volatile pre-retirement and early retirement periods. Regular reviews of your retirement plan will enable you to make timely adjustments and maintain a secure financial foundation. Your approach should be dynamic, evolving with market changes, policy adjustments, and personal circumstances.

Never underestimate the power of professional advice. A comprehensive financial plan created and monitored by a trusted advisor is an invaluable tool, offering stability, clarity, and peace of mind. Remember, retirement is a marathon, not a sprint, and a sound strategy is crucial.

3.3 Roth Conversions

Converting traditional IRA assets to a Roth IRA, often called a Roth conversion, presents a strategic opportunity to manage your retirement tax burden. This involves transferring funds from a traditional IRA, where contributions are tax-deductible but withdrawals are taxed in retirement, to a Roth IRA, where contributions aren't tax-deductible but withdrawals are tax-free in retirement. The immediate tax cost is a key consideration, as you'll pay income tax on the converted amount in the year of the conversion.

However, the long-term benefits can significantly outweigh this upfront tax liability, particularly for those who anticipate being in a higher tax bracket in retirement than they are now. This is a crucial point to consider: your future tax bracket is a major factor in determining the viability of a Roth conversion. Carefully assess your current and projected income to make an informed decision. Consider seeking professional financial advice for a personalized analysis if your circumstances are complex. Remember, accurate forecasting of future tax rates is inherently uncertain due to changing legislation and economic conditions.

The decision to convert hinges on many individual factors. Your age plays a significant role. Younger individuals who have a longer time horizon for growth and potentially lower current income may find this a more attractive approach, allowing the converted assets to grow tax-free for a longer period. Older individuals approaching retirement need a different level of assessment, weighing the immediate tax implications against the potentially limited timeframe for tax-free growth. Not only age but also your overall financial situation must be considered carefully. The amount you convert should align with your current financial capacity to pay the immediate tax liability. Avoid converting funds that could significantly strain your current finances or jeopardize other important financial goals. It is prudent to only convert what you can comfortably afford. It is also wise to diversify your retirement savings, so that not all your retirement eggs are in one basket. This is particularly relevant for those nearing retirement, to maintain liquidity and minimize risk.

Understanding the tax implications is paramount. While withdrawals from a Roth IRA are tax-free, the conversion itself is a taxable event. The tax will be calculated based on your marginal tax bracket in the year of the conversion. Therefore, understanding your current and projected tax brackets is vital. This requires meticulous planning and attention to detail. You must also understand the rules governing Roth conversions.

Furthermore, Roth conversions offer significant flexibility. You aren't obliged to convert your entire traditional IRA balance at once. Consider performing partial conversions over several years to better manage the immediate tax liability and spread the tax burden. This approach offers better control over your taxable income and provides a greater degree of flexibility to adjust to changing circumstances. This strategy can be especially useful if you expect your income to fluctuate significantly over time.

Finally, remember that tax laws are subject to change. What is advantageous today may not be so tomorrow. Consulting with a qualified financial advisor is strongly recommended to help navigate these complexities. They can assist in creating a personalized retirement plan that incorporates Roth conversions effectively, considering your specific circumstances, tax implications, and long-term goals. A professional can help you stay abreast of changes to tax legislation, and help you avoid any costly errors. Their expertise will ensure you are making sound financial decisions aligned with your individual financial situation and long-term objectives. Seeking professional guidance is undeniably invaluable.

3.4 Tax-Advantaged Accounts

Tax-advantaged accounts offer significant benefits for retirement planning, allowing you to grow your savings while minimizing your tax burden. Understanding the nuances of these accounts is crucial for maximizing your retirement wealth. Different accounts cater to different needs and financial situations, so careful consideration is key. For example, a traditional IRA allows for pre-tax contributions, reducing your current taxable income. However, withdrawals in retirement are taxed as ordinary income. Conversely, a Roth IRA involves after-tax contributions, but withdrawals in retirement are tax-free, providing a substantial advantage.

The 401(k) plan, often offered through employers, provides another avenue for tax-advantaged savings. Many employers match a portion of employee contributions, essentially giving you free money toward retirement. Similar to traditional IRAs, contributions are pre-tax, reducing your current taxable income. However, withdrawals are subject to income tax upon distribution. Careful consideration should be given to your employer's matching contribution and the plan's investment options.

Health Savings Accounts (HSAs) offer a triple tax advantage: contributions are tax-deductible, earnings grow tax-free, and withdrawals for qualified medical expenses are tax-free. HSAs are particularly beneficial for those enrolled in high-deductible health plans, allowing you to save for medical expenses while enjoying significant tax benefits. It's important to remember that HSAs are not just for immediate medical needs; the money can grow tax-free for future medical expenses in retirement.

Choosing between a traditional and Roth IRA, or even a combination of both, hinges on several factors. Your current tax bracket, projected future tax bracket, and risk tolerance all play a significant role in determining the most advantageous strategy. If you expect to be in a higher tax bracket in retirement, a Roth IRA might be more beneficial. Conversely, a lower future tax bracket might favor a traditional IRA. Consulting with a financial advisor can help navigate these complexities.

Beyond the widely known accounts, other tax-advantaged options exist. For example, 529 plans offer tax benefits for saving for higher education expenses. While not directly for retirement, they can significantly reduce the financial burden of college, freeing up resources for retirement savings. This can provide a buffer against unexpected expenses later in life. It's crucial to understand the rules and regulations governing these accounts.

Effective management of tax-advantaged accounts requires ongoing monitoring and adjustment. Regularly reviewing your investment allocation and contribution strategies is essential to ensure they remain aligned with your retirement goals and overall financial plan. As your circumstances change, so should your investment strategy. Don't be afraid to adjust your approach as needed. This proactive approach will keep you on track toward a financially secure retirement.

Remember that the information provided here is for general guidance only and does not constitute financial advice. The specific suitability of any tax-advantaged account depends on individual circumstances and financial objectives. Always consult with a qualified financial advisor or tax professional before making any investment decisions. They can help you tailor a strategy that aligns perfectly with your unique financial situation and retirement goals. Don't hesitate to seek professional help to navigate the complexities of retirement planning. Your future self will thank you for it.

Proper planning and careful consideration of your options will greatly impact your financial wellbeing in retirement. Seeking expert advice is crucial to avoid costly mistakes and maximize your retirement income. Proactive planning today will ensure a more comfortable and secure retirement tomorrow. This proactive approach minimizes the risks and maximizes your long-term gains. Taking control of your financial future is essential for a rewarding retirement.

It's important to understand the rules and regulations surrounding tax-advantaged accounts. These rules can change, so staying informed is crucial. Familiarize yourself with contribution limits, withdrawal penalties, and other relevant factors to ensure compliance. Regularly reviewing your accounts and making adjustments as needed is a key element in maximizing their benefits. This involves not just tracking investment performance but also verifying your contributions and withdrawals remain aligned with regulations.

Finally, remember that a comprehensive retirement plan includes more than just tax-advantaged accounts. It's essential to create a holistic strategy that addresses all aspects of your financial well-being in retirement. Consider factors like health care costs, debt management, and lifestyle adjustments to ensure a comfortable and financially secure retirement. This combined approach will set you on the right path for a rewarding retirement experience. Planning ahead is not merely advisable; it's essential to your success.

3.5 Account Management

Regularly reviewing your retirement accounts isn't just about checking balances; it's about actively managing your financial future. Think of it as tending a garden – consistent attention ensures healthy growth. Neglect it, and weeds (unforeseen expenses, poor investment choices) can quickly overtake your carefully planted seeds (savings and investments). This proactive approach will safeguard your retirement's financial health, enabling you to enjoy the fruits of your labor.

Understanding your asset allocation is paramount. This isn't a set-it-

and-forget-it proposition. Market conditions shift, your risk tolerance might change with age, and your goals may evolve. Perhaps your initial strategy prioritized aggressive growth, but as retirement nears, a more conservative approach might be warranted. Regularly rebalancing your portfolio – adjusting the proportions of stocks, bonds, and other assets to align with your updated risk profile – is crucial for mitigating risk and maintaining a healthy balance. Don't be afraid to seek professional advice; a financial advisor can provide personalized guidance tailored to your individual circumstances.

Withdrawal strategies require careful consideration. How and when you access your retirement funds directly impacts your longevity of funds. There's no one-size-fits-all answer; the optimal strategy depends on factors like your age, health, anticipated expenses, and the type of accounts you hold. Early withdrawals from tax-advantaged accounts might incur penalties, while systematic withdrawals from a diversified portfolio can offer stability. A well-structured plan minimizes tax implications and safeguards against unforeseen circumstances, providing a consistent stream of income. This ensures your retirement fund's longevity.

Consider the power of tax-efficient withdrawals. Understanding the tax implications of withdrawing from different accounts is crucial for maximizing your after-tax income. For example, strategically withdrawing from Roth IRAs, where distributions are tax-free, can significantly increase your disposable income during retirement. By carefully planning your withdrawals, you can minimize your overall tax burden and retain more of your hard-earned savings. This requires thorough knowledge and potentially professional advice.

Don't underestimate the importance of monitoring fees. High fees can stealthily erode your retirement savings over time, significantly impacting your overall returns. Regularly review the expense ratios of your investments, comparing them to similar options. Choosing low-cost index funds or ETFs can drastically reduce these costs, allowing your investments to grow more efficiently. Remember even small percentages add up significantly over decades.

Keep an eye on your beneficiary designations. Ensure that your beneficiaries are correctly listed on all your retirement accounts. Regularly reviewing and updating this information is crucial, especially after major life events like marriage, divorce, or the birth of a child. Keeping your paperwork current ensures your assets are distributed according to your wishes, preventing potential complications and disputes for your loved ones. This simple act provides peace of mind.

Finally, remember that your retirement plan is a dynamic document, not a static one. Life throws curveballs; unexpected job losses, medical emergencies, and changing family dynamics can all impact your retirement plan. Regularly review and adjust your strategy to account for these changes. Flexibility and adaptability are key to weathering life's storms and ensuring a secure and comfortable retirement. Your retirement plan should be a living document, adapting with you, ensuring financial security and future peace of mind. Don't hesitate to seek professional advice when needed. This ongoing adaptation is crucial to secure your financial future.

4 Chapter 4: Managing Debt

Debt can feel like an insurmountable obstacle, especially when planning for retirement. However, proactive management is key to securing a financially comfortable future. Don't let debt derail your dreams; instead, view it as a challenge to overcome, one that, with careful planning, you can conquer. Ignoring debt only allows it to grow, compounding interest and eating away at your potential retirement savings. Taking control is empowering.

Prioritize high-interest debts. Credit card debt, often exceeding 15% interest, demands immediate attention. Aggressive strategies, like the debt snowball or avalanche methods, can significantly reduce this burden. The snowball method focuses on paying off the smallest debt first for psychological momentum, while the avalanche method prioritizes the debt with the highest interest rate for maximum financial savings. Both methods necessitate a disciplined approach, requiring diligent tracking and consistent payments. Choose the method that best suits your personality and financial situation.

Consider refinancing your mortgage. A lower interest rate on your mortgage can free up significant cash flow each month, enabling you to allocate more towards retirement savings or other pressing debts.

Shop around for competitive rates; don't just accept the first offer you receive. Furthermore, investigate options like a 15-year mortgage, although requiring larger monthly payments, this can substantially reduce long-term interest costs, potentially saving you thousands of dollars over the life of the loan.

Explore debt consolidation. Consolidating multiple debts into a single loan, ideally with a lower interest rate, simplifies payments and can provide a clearer picture of your overall financial situation. Be aware of the terms and conditions of any consolidation loan; ensure it truly benefits you in the long run and doesn't merely postpone the issue. Carefully consider the implications; sometimes consolidating can extend your repayment period, increasing the total interest paid. Always compare options thoroughly.

Negotiate with creditors. You might be surprised at how willing creditors are to work with you. Explain your financial situation honestly and propose a modified repayment plan, perhaps reducing monthly payments or temporarily suspending interest. This strategy requires clear communication and documentation of your financial hardship; be prepared to provide proof of income and expenses. Remember, a timely and respectful conversation can often lead to more favorable terms.

Develop a comprehensive budget. A detailed budget is crucial for managing debt effectively and achieving your retirement goals. Track all income and expenses meticulously, identifying areas where you can reduce spending. Allocate funds specifically for debt repayment, ensuring it's treated as a non-negotiable expense. A well-structured budget will give you the transparency and control necessary to make informed financial decisions. Make it a habit to review and adjust your budget regularly to reflect changes in your income or expenses.

Don't rely solely on quick fixes. While strategies like debt consolidation and negotiation can provide immediate relief, they are not long-term solutions unless accompanied by sustainable lifestyle changes and responsible financial habits. Addressing the underlying causes of your debt is essential to prevent future accumulation. Avoid impulsive spending and develop a plan for managing your finances responsibly. This involves building an emergency fund to handle unexpected expenses, avoiding further debt accumulation, and steadily paying down existing debts.

Seek professional advice. If you're overwhelmed by debt or struggling to develop a plan, don't hesitate to seek professional guidance. A financial advisor can provide personalized strategies tailored to your specific circumstances. They can help you create a comprehensive debt reduction plan, navigate complex financial issues, and develop a long-term strategy to ensure a secure retirement. Their expertise can prove invaluable in making informed decisions and avoiding costly mistakes.

Remember, managing debt is a journey, not a sprint. It requires patience, persistence, and a commitment to making positive changes. Be kind to yourself during the process; celebrate small victories and remain focused on your ultimate goal of a secure and comfortable retirement. By implementing these strategies and maintaining a proactive approach, you can effectively manage your debt and create a solid foundation for your financial future. Ultimately, taking control of your finances now will yield significant rewards in your retirement years, freeing you to enjoy the fruits of your labor without the constant burden of debt.

4.1 Debt Reduction

Tackling debt before retirement is crucial; it's not merely about having enough money saved, but also about having enough available money. High-interest debt, like credit card balances, acts as a constant drain, siphoning off funds that could otherwise be invested for growth or used to cover living expenses in retirement. The sooner you address this, the better positioned you'll be for a financially secure retirement. One effective strategy is the debt snowball method. This involves listing your debts from smallest to largest balance, regardless of interest rate. Focus all extra funds on paying off the smallest debt first. The psychological boost of achieving that first win is incredibly motivating, providing momentum to tackle larger debts. This method isn't mathematically optimal, prioritizing psychological satisfaction over pure efficiency. However, the increased motivation it provides often leads to faster overall debt reduction.

Conversely, the debt avalanche method prioritizes debts with the highest interest rates. Mathematically, this is the most efficient way to minimize the total interest paid over time. You aggressively attack the debt costing you the most money, aiming to reduce the overall long-term cost. While this method is more financially sound, the slower initial progress might dampen motivation for some individuals. Choose the method that best suits your personality and financial discipline.

Beyond choosing a repayment strategy, actively seeking ways to reduce your monthly expenses is vital. This might involve reviewing subscriptions, cutting back on non-essential spending, or even renegotiating bills, such as your phone or internet plan. Even small savings add up over time, contributing significantly to your debt reduction efforts. Consider using budgeting apps to track spending and identify areas for improvement. Remember, financial discipline is key here. Every dollar saved is a dollar closer to a debt-free future.

Debt consolidation can be a powerful tool, especially if you have multiple high-interest debts. This involves taking out a single loan with a lower interest rate to pay off all your existing debts. This simplifies your repayments into a single, more manageable monthly payment. Be cautious, though. Ensure the terms of the consolidation loan are favorable and compare interest rates offered by different lenders before making a decision. Avoid consolidating only to run up new debt on the old cards - use this opportunity to truly alter your spending habits.

Negotiating with creditors can also yield surprising results. Many creditors are willing to work with individuals facing financial hardship. Explain your situation honestly and propose a modified repayment plan, such as a reduced monthly payment or a temporary period of forbearance. This demonstrates your commitment to repaying your debt and can prevent negative impacts on your credit score. Document every conversation and agreement in writing for your records.

Finally, consider a financial advisor's perspective. They can provide personalized guidance based on your specific financial situation, helping you navigate complex debt management strategies, and helping you create a personalized debt reduction plan. They can offer objective insights and support, enhancing the probability of your success in achieving a debt-free retirement. Their expertise can make the process less overwhelming and more effective. Remember, professional help is often invaluable, and the cost is often far outweighed by the benefits obtained. Seeking help is a sign of strength, not weakness. The investment in professional advice is an investment in your future.

4.2 Mortgage Strategies

Your mortgage is likely your largest debt, significantly impacting your retirement readiness. Understanding and strategically managing it is crucial. Don't let it derail your golden years. A poorly managed mortgage can eat away at your retirement savings, leaving you with less to enjoy during your well-deserved break.

One primary strategy involves refinancing. This process entails replacing your existing mortgage with a new one, often at a lower interest rate. Lower interest rates translate to lower monthly payments, freeing up funds for retirement investments or other crucial needs. Before refinancing, meticulously compare rates and terms from different lenders. Factor in closing costs; a lower interest rate might not be worthwhile if the closing costs outweigh the savings over the life of the loan. Consider your financial situation carefully; are you financially stable enough to handle unforeseen expenses from closing costs, and would refinancing align with your long-term financial goals?

Another critical aspect is paying extra toward your principal. Even small additional payments can dramatically shorten your loan term and substantially reduce the total interest paid over the life of the loan. Direct any extra funds towards your principal balance to optimize your payment and minimize the overall cost. This is particularly effective in the early years of your mortgage, when a larger portion of your payments goes towards interest. Think about how much you are comfortable paying extra monthly and how much it will shorten your loan. An amortization schedule, easily obtained online or from your lender, will show the precise impact of extra payments on your principal and interest.

If you anticipate retirement within the next few years, carefully examine the potential tax implications of your mortgage interest deduction. This deduction can be significant for many homeowners, reducing their overall tax liability. However, your deduction will decrease as you pay down your principal. Consider a strategy to balance tax savings with the advantages of paying off your mortgage sooner rather than later. Planning how your mortgage will interact with your other retirement investments and how that could affect your tax bracket is a sensible approach.

Explore the possibility of a reverse mortgage. This option, suitable for homeowners 62 or older, allows you to access a portion of your home equity as tax-free cash. The loan becomes due when you sell your home or pass away. However, this approach has significant risks. It's crucial to fully understand the terms and conditions, and to carefully consider the potential impact on your heirs. This is not the right choice for everyone, so thoroughly explore your available options to discover what is best for your situation.

Finally, remember your mortgage is a significant part of your overall financial picture during retirement. Its proper management is a critical element of your overall retirement plan. Consider consulting with a financial advisor experienced in retirement planning to receive personalized guidance. They can help you navigate the complexities of mortgage strategies and create a tailored plan to help you reach your retirement goals, and even to make sure that you have some emergency money set aside for any unexpected expenses. This integrated approach, ensuring your mortgage aligns with your broader financial strategy, is essential for a secure and comfortable retirement. Don't underestimate the power of proactive planning and professional guidance. Your future self will thank you.

5 Chapter 5: Tax Optimization

Tax optimization is crucial for maximizing your retirement income. Understanding available deductions and credits can significantly reduce your tax burden, leaving more money for your enjoyment. Don't overlook the power of tax planning; it's not just about compliance, it's about strategically minimizing your tax liability to preserve your hard-earned savings.

Many retirees are unaware of the tax advantages specifically designed for them. For instance, the standard deduction is often higher for those over 65, and additional deductions may be available for medical expenses exceeding a certain percentage of your adjusted gross income. Proactively seeking out these deductions and keeping meticulous records are critical for successful tax optimization. Consult a tax professional to ensure you are taking full advantage of every applicable deduction. Remember, even small deductions add up over time, making a substantial difference in your overall tax liability.

Beyond deductions, consider exploring tax credits. These credits directly reduce your tax owed, offering a more significant impact than deductions. Certain credits, such as the Saver's Credit, can benefit those contributing to retirement accounts, making them doubly beneficial. Research various credits available to retirees and those with specific circumstances, as eligibility criteria can change annually. Professional guidance is essential for navigating this complex area and maximizing your potential tax savings. Don't hesitate to seek assistance; the expertise is invaluable.

Careful estate planning is just as essential as managing your taxes during your retirement years. This involves making informed decisions about your will, trusts, and beneficiary designations to minimize estate taxes and ensure a smooth transition for your heirs. Proper planning minimizes potential tax liabilities for your beneficiaries, protecting their inheritance and preserving the legacy you worked to build.

One often-overlooked aspect of tax optimization involves charitable giving. Strategic charitable donations can offer significant tax benefits while supporting causes you care about. Donating appreciated assets, rather than cash, can minimize capital gains taxes. Discuss charitable giving strategies with your tax advisor to explore tax-efficient ways to support your chosen charities. It's a win-win scenario, combining philanthropy with smart tax planning.

Beyond the traditional tax strategies, consider the impact of your state taxes. Many states also have deductions and credits specifically for retirees. Understanding the nuances of both federal and state tax laws is essential to comprehensive tax optimization. Don't limit your planning to federal taxes; explore state-specific opportunities for further minimizing your overall tax liability. A holistic approach is key to achieving optimal results.

Finally, remember that tax laws are dynamic and subject to change. Stay informed about current tax legislation and seek regular advice from a qualified tax professional. Regular reviews of your tax strategy will ensure that you remain compliant and take advantage of any changes that could benefit you. Annual tax planning sessions should be a non-negotiable element of your retirement strategy, as this proactive approach guarantees you're always on the right path to tax optimization. Don't treat this as a one-time event, rather integrate it as a key component of your ongoing retirement financial planning. The small amount of time and effort now, can save you significant amounts later on. This vigilance is an investment in your financial future.

5.1 Tax Deductions

Many retirees overlook significant tax deductions that could substantially reduce their tax burden. Understanding these deductions is crucial for maximizing your retirement income and ensuring a comfortable lifestyle. For instance, the deduction for qualified charitable contributions can be substantial, particularly if you itemize instead of taking the standard deduction. This allows you to deduct cash contributions up to 60% of your adjusted gross income (AGI). Don't forget, this applies to contributions to qualifying charities; carefully verify this status before contributing.

Taxpayers aged 65 or older may be able to take a higher standard deduction. This often makes itemizing less beneficial, but understanding your eligibility is key, especially considering interactions with other deductions. Remember, you must always compare the standard deduction with the total of your itemized deductions; only claim the larger amount. This careful comparison is crucial for effective tax planning. Medical expenses can also offer significant tax relief. While you can only deduct expenses exceeding 7.5% of your adjusted gross income (AGI), substantial medical bills from procedures or ongoing care, such as those for chronic illnesses, can significantly impact this threshold. Keep meticulous records, including receipts and documentation; these documents prove crucial for claiming the deduction. Remember to consult a tax professional for clarification on eligible medical expenses.

State and local taxes (SALT) deductions are often a significant portion of many taxpayers' deductions. However, there are limitations to consider. The 2017 Tax Cuts and Jobs Act imposed a $10,000 limit on the combined deduction for state and local property, income, and sales taxes. Before making assumptions about your state and local tax deduction, research your state's tax laws and any applicable limits. This knowledge helps ensure you claim the correct amount.

Homeowners can benefit from mortgage interest deductions. This deduction applies to interest paid on mortgages up to $750,000 (for loans originated after December 15, 2017). Keep detailed records of your mortgage interest payments, as this is a crucial element of maximizing your tax benefits and claiming the proper amount on your tax return. It's always advisable to review this annually, as changes in your mortgage could influence your deduction eligibility.

For those with significant retirement account distributions, there might be opportunities to deduct specific expenses related to managing these funds. Fees associated with professional financial advice or investment management can sometimes be tax-deductible under certain conditions. However, these situations are usually complex and require a careful review of your specific circumstances. Therefore, consulting a tax professional is highly recommended to understand the precise requirements and eligibility criteria for these deductions.

Self-employment income often comes with numerous tax deductions. These can include deductions for home office expenses, if you have a dedicated workspace, business expenses directly related to your work, and health insurance premiums if you are self-employed. Be aware of the specific documentation needed to support each deduction. Carefully categorizing and tracking these expenses is paramount for accurate and efficient tax filing.

Beyond itemized deductions, consider exploring tax credits specifically designed for seniors. These can directly reduce your tax liability, and some are available only to seniors, offering further tax savings opportunities. Researching available credits–such as the Retirement Savings Contributions Credit–is essential, as it can directly lower your tax bill, unlike deductions which only reduce your taxable income. It's advisable to research state tax credits specific to your residence as well, as these often complement federal credits.

Remember, careful record-keeping is paramount. Maintaining organized records of your income, expenses, and supporting documentation is vital to successfully claiming all available deductions. This meticulous record-keeping protects against potential audit issues and helps you maximize your tax savings. Organizing your files in a clear and easily accessible manner greatly simplifies the process when tax season arrives.

Finally, don't hesitate to seek professional advice. A qualified tax advisor can help you navigate the complexities of tax laws, identify all applicable deductions and credits, and ensure you're taking full advantage of available tax benefits. This professional assistance is often invaluable, particularly given the intricate nature of tax regulations and the substantial financial implications of accurately claiming deductions and credits. A proactive approach to tax planning significantly enhances your retirement security and financial well-being.

5.2 Tax Credits

Tax credits offer a powerful tool for reducing your tax liability during retirement, potentially significantly boosting your retirement income. Unlike deductions, which reduce your taxable income, credits directly reduce the amount of tax you owe, dollar for dollar. This makes them particularly valuable, especially for retirees on fixed incomes. Understanding which credits you qualify for is crucial.

The most widely known retirement-related tax credit is the Saver's Credit. This credit is designed to assist middle\item and lower-income taxpayers in saving for retirement. The amount of the credit depends on your adjusted gross income (AGI) and the amount you contribute to a retirement account like a traditional IRA or 401(k). The credit percentage varies, with higher percentages available to those with lower incomes. It's important to note that contribution limits exist for the Saver's Credit; exceeding those limits won't increase the amount you receive. Careful planning and understanding your contribution limits are essential to maximizing this valuable credit. Consult the IRS website or a tax professional for the most up-to-date information regarding AGI thresholds and contribution limits.

Beyond the Saver's Credit, other credits may apply depending on your individual circumstances. For instance, if you are a senior citizen who incurred significant medical expenses, you might qualify for the credit for medical expenses. This credit allows you to deduct medical expenses exceeding 7.5% of your AGI. While this isn't strictly a retirement-specific credit, its relevance to retirees is undeniable, given that healthcare costs often represent a considerable expense in later life. Accurately tracking and documenting these expenses throughout the year is key to claiming this credit successfully. Maintaining detailed receipts and records is crucial for a smooth tax filing process.

Another potential credit worth exploring is the Earned Income Tax Credit (EITC), though eligibility rules may limit this for retirees. While primarily designed for working individuals with low to moderate incomes, some retirees, particularly those with part-time employment, could potentially qualify. The EITC offers substantial tax relief, reducing tax burdens and helping to supplement retirement income. Understanding the EITC's stringent eligibility requirements is essential, including income limits, number of qualifying children, and work-related criteria. The EITC's guidelines change annually, so it is vital to consult the latest IRS publications or seek professional guidance to ascertain your eligibility.

Furthermore, consider the potential tax credits related to healthcare costs. These credits are especially relevant in retirement when healthcare expenses often skyrocket. The specifics of these credits vary greatly and depend on your health insurance coverage and other health-related circumstances. It's crucial to investigate these options thoroughly, as they might drastically reduce your overall tax burden. This investigation often requires a careful review of your insurance policies, medical bills, and other supporting documentation.

Don't overlook the importance of accurate record-keeping. Meticulously maintaining records of all relevant expenses, contributions, and income sources is vital for claiming any tax credit successfully. This includes receipts, bank statements, and tax forms. Organized documentation significantly simplifies the tax filing process and reduces the risk of errors or omissions, which can delay refunds or even lead to penalties. Consider using a tax software program or consulting with a qualified tax professional to ensure accuracy and maximize your tax credit claims. Remember, a small oversight can cost you significant savings. Proactive planning and attention to detail will pay substantial dividends.

Finally, keep in mind that tax laws are subject to change. Regularly reviewing updates from the IRS and seeking professional tax advice are essential to remain compliant and take advantage of all available credits. Tax laws are complex and their implications for your financial situation should be carefully considered. Proactive and informed tax planning is an investment in your financial well-being, ensuring you receive the maximum benefits available to you. By staying informed and seeking expert guidance, you can make the most of tax credits and safeguard your financial security in retirement.

5.3 Estate Planning

Estate planning is often overlooked until it's too late, yet it's a cornerstone of securing your retirement wealth and minimizing tax burdens for your heirs. Procrastination can lead to unintended consequences, including significant tax liabilities for your loved ones and potential legal battles over your assets. Don't let this happen to you. Careful planning now safeguards your legacy and provides peace of mind.

A well-structured estate plan isn't just for the ultra-wealthy; it's a vital component of responsible financial planning for everyone, regardless of net worth. It ensures your wishes are carried out according to your plan and not subject to the whims of the court system. This translates to minimizing legal fees and family disputes, preserving your hard-earned wealth for those you designate.

Consider the distribution of your assets. A simple will might seem sufficient, but it may not address all potential scenarios. For example, a will only dictates how your assets are distributed after your death, and doesn't necessarily cover how those assets will be managed while you are still alive but incapacitated. This is where a more comprehensive approach such as a living trust becomes relevant.

A living trust, unlike a will, takes effect while you are still alive. It allows for the designation of a trustee who manages your assets according to your instructions, even if you become incapacitated. This protects your assets and ensures continuity of management. The specific terms of the trust—who manages assets and when they are distributed—are entirely within your control, preventing potential conflicts later. It's advisable to consult with an estate attorney to draft a trust that accurately reflects your wishes.

Beyond trusts and wills, consider powers of attorney. These legal documents authorize someone to act on your behalf if you're unable to manage your own affairs. A durable power of attorney remains in effect even if you become incapacitated, allowing a designated person to make financial and healthcare decisions for you. A healthcare power of attorney, or advance directive, is crucial in determining your healthcare wishes should you become unable to communicate them. This is where you can specify your preference for life support or other end-of-life decisions, ensuring your comfort and wishes are respected.

Careful estate planning also minimizes tax liability for your heirs. Understanding the implications of estate and inheritance taxes is critical. Depending on your location and the value of your estate, significant taxes may be levied upon your death. Strategic planning, often involving the use of trusts and other tax-advantaged vehicles, can significantly reduce this burden. This reduces the financial strain on your beneficiaries during a difficult time, allowing them to focus on grieving rather than dealing with complex financial issues. For instance, strategically gifting assets during your lifetime—within annual gift tax limits—can substantially reduce your taxable estate.

Finally, regularly review and update your estate plan. Life changes—marriage, divorce, birth of children, significant asset acquisitions or losses—all necessitate reviewing your plan to ensure it aligns with your current circumstances and goals. This prevents potential legal and tax complications down the line, ensuring the smooth and efficient transfer of your assets to your chosen beneficiaries. Your financial advisor and attorney can help you monitor and amend your plan as needed. Regular reviews are a crucial step to maintain the effectiveness of your estate plan in preserving the legacy you desire. Remember, proactive estate planning is not merely about minimizing taxes; it is about securing your family's financial future and ensuring a peaceful transition during a difficult time. It's an investment in peace of mind, safeguarding your legacy and your family's future. The work involved may seem daunting, but the benefits far outweigh the effort.

6 Chapter 6: Healthcare Costs

Healthcare is a significant, often unpredictable, expense in retirement. Failing to adequately plan for these costs can severely impact your financial security, potentially jeopardizing the comfortable retirement you've worked so hard to achieve. Understanding Medicare, supplemental insurance options, and long-term care planning is crucial. Don't underestimate the potential burden of medical bills; proactive planning is key.

Medicare, the federal health insurance program for those 65 and older, is a foundation, but it's not all-inclusive. It covers a portion of your medical expenses, but significant out-of-pocket costs remain. Understanding Medicare Parts A, B, C, and D – their coverage, deductibles, and premiums – is the first step. Each part plays a distinct role, and careful consideration of your health needs will determine which plan best suits your circumstances. Research your options thoroughly; don't rely solely on what you've heard anecdotally.

Consider supplemental insurance, often called Medigap, to help fill the gaps left by original Medicare. These plans are sold by private companies and cover expenses Medicare doesn't, such as co-payments, deductibles, and coinsurance. The cost of Medigap policies varies, influenced by your age, location, and the plan's coverage. Carefully analyze the coverage provided by each plan to ensure it meets your individual healthcare needs and budget constraints. Choosing wisely will minimize unexpected medical expenses.

Long-term care, including nursing home stays or in-home assistance, is another significant cost that many overlook. The expense of such care can quickly deplete retirement savings. Long-term care insurance is designed to help offset these costs, but it's essential to secure coverage early, as premiums increase with age. Alternatively, you may consider exploring other financial options, such as reverse mortgages or Medicaid, for funding long-term care. Weigh all your options carefully and select a solution that best protects your financial future.

Prescription drug costs can also quickly add up, especially with multiple medications. Explore options to reduce these costs. Consider using a mail-order pharmacy for cost savings, negotiating prices with your pharmacy, or checking for manufacturer coupons or discount cards. Look into your Medicare Part D plan's formulary to understand which medications are covered and at what cost. Take the time to compare plans and find the most cost-effective option. Don't be afraid to use resources designed to help you navigate this complexity.

Finally, actively managing your healthcare costs requires consistent effort and vigilance. Regular checkups, preventive care, and adopting a healthy lifestyle can help avoid more expensive health issues in the future. Maintaining a healthy lifestyle will help reduce your long-term healthcare costs. Remember, preventative healthcare is an investment.

Budgeting for healthcare expenses in retirement isn't just about having the money readily available; it's about building a comprehensive financial strategy. This necessitates understanding your personal healthcare situation, researching potential costs, and securing appropriate insurance coverage. This proactive approach will safeguard your financial security during your retirement. Never assume adequate coverage exists, explore all available options.

6.1 Medicare Basics

Understanding Medicare is crucial for securing your financial future in retirement. It's a complex system, but grasping the fundamentals can save you significant money and stress. Medicare isn't simply one program; it's a collection of federally-funded health insurance programs for people aged 65 and over, as well as some younger individuals with disabilities. Knowing the different parts is the first step.

Part A, often called hospital insurance, primarily covers inpatient hospital stays, skilled nursing facility care, hospice, and some home healthcare. Most people don't pay a premium for Part A because they've earned enough work credits during their working years. However, there are copayments and deductibles involved, so understanding those limits is essential. Failure to do so could lead to unexpected out-of-pocket expenses. Careful review of your Part A coverage is paramount.

Part B, or medical insurance, helps cover doctor visits, outpatient care, medical supplies, and preventive services. Unlike Part A, Part B does require a monthly premium, the cost of which varies based on income. The higher your income, the more you'll typically pay. Understanding the cost-sharing responsibilities, like the annual deductible and co-insurance, is critical for budget planning. Failing to do so could lead to financial difficulties when medical expenses arise unexpectedly. This aspect often requires careful and proactive planning.

Part D covers prescription drugs. It's administered by private insurance companies that Medicare has approved. The monthly premium varies depending on the plan you choose and your income. Medicare Part D plans have a complex structure involving deductibles, premiums, and coverage gaps known as the "donut hole," where you pay a higher percentage of your prescription costs. Navigating this requires careful comparison-shopping among plans. Failing to understand these complexities can lead to substantial overspending on medications. An active approach is necessary, not a passive one.

Medicare Advantage (Part C) offers an alternative way to receive your Medicare coverage. These are plans offered by private companies that provide all of your Parts A and B benefits, and often include Part D as well. Medicare Advantage plans may offer extra benefits, such as vision, hearing, or dental coverage, that Original Medicare doesn't. However, these plans often have restrictions, such as a narrower network of doctors and hospitals you can use. Therefore, selecting the right plan requires considerable attention to your needs. Choosing a Medicare Advantage plan without thoroughly considering these factors can leave individuals with limited healthcare options. This should be approached with extreme care and planning.

Understanding these components of Medicare, including deductibles, co-pays, and premiums associated with each part, is essential. This knowledge empowers you to plan your retirement budget effectively. Moreover, you can take advantage of enrollment periods and plan changes to optimize your healthcare coverage. Annual review of your plan, given the changes that occur, is essential to maintain a financially secure retirement. A proactive approach ensures you receive the maximum benefits from this complex system.

Supplementing your Medicare coverage with a Medigap or supplemental insurance plan is strongly recommended. These plans help cover some of the out-of-pocket costs, like co-pays and deductibles, that Original Medicare doesn't. Choosing the right Medigap plan depends on your individual needs and budget. There are ten standardized Medigap plans (A-N, excluding M), each with a different set of benefits. Careful comparison-shopping is crucial to find a plan that suits your financial situation and health requirements. A thorough understanding of your medical history and anticipated health needs is crucial before committing to a plan.

Finally, remember to enroll in Medicare. You'll want to enroll during your Initial Enrollment Period (IEP), which typically begins three months before your 65th birthday and ends three months after. Missing your IEP can result in significant penalties. Staying informed and understanding your options helps you navigate the complexities of Medicare effectively. Proactive planning will minimize financial surprises and maximize your healthcare benefits, leading to a more secure and enjoyable retirement. Planning early gives you time to understand the available options and pick the perfect option that suits you, giving you peace of mind and financial security. This is paramount.

6.2 Supplemental Insurance

Medicare, while providing a crucial foundation, often leaves gaps in coverage. This necessitates supplemental insurance, a topic many retirees find daunting but essential to navigate. Understanding the nuances of Medigap plans, Medicare Advantage plans, and Part D prescription drug coverage is vital for minimizing out-of-pocket expenses and ensuring comprehensive healthcare protection during retirement. Failing to plan for these costs can significantly erode your carefully accumulated retirement savings.

Numerous Medigap plans exist, each offering a different level of coverage. Plan G, for example, covers most Medicare cost-sharing expenses, including co-pays and deductibles. However, it doesn't cover the Part B annual deductible. Plan F, a more comprehensive option (though less common now due to new regulations), covers that deductible as well. Understanding your individual healthcare needs and budget is key to choosing the right Medigap plan. Don't rush into a decision; thoroughly research your options and compare plans from multiple insurers. Consider your health status, predicted healthcare needs, and financial resources to make an informed choice.

Medicare Advantage plans, offered by private insurance companies, provide an alternative to Original Medicare. These plans often include prescription drug coverage (Part D), and some offer additional benefits like vision and dental care. While potentially offering lower monthly premiums than Medigap plans, the level of out-of-pocket costs can vary significantly among different plans and providers. Selecting the right Medicare Advantage plan necessitates a careful analysis of its network of doctors and hospitals, ensuring your preferred healthcare providers are included within the plan. Carefully evaluate potential deductibles, co-pays, and out-of-pocket maximums to ensure alignment with your financial capabilities and health requirements.

Prescription drug coverage, or Part D, is crucial for managing medication costs, often a significant expense in retirement. Part D plans vary substantially in their formularies (list of covered drugs), premiums, and cost-sharing. Some plans feature lower premiums but higher costs for specific medications. A thorough understanding of your medication regimen is essential for choosing a plan. Utilize the Medicare Plan Finder or consult with a qualified insurance agent to evaluate available plans and their respective costs related to your medications. The cost implications of selecting a plan that doesn't cover your necessary medications could be substantial over time.

Choosing the right supplemental insurance requires careful consideration. Many resources, including Medicare.gov and independent insurance brokers, can provide assistance. Seek professional guidance to determine the best option tailored to your individual circumstances. Don't hesitate to compare plans across multiple insurers to secure the most comprehensive coverage at the most competitive price. Remember, your health is a significant aspect of your retirement, so comprehensive insurance is a necessary investment.

Unexpected health crises, such as prolonged hospital stays or extensive rehabilitation needs, can devastate retirement finances. Planning for the possibility of long-term care is prudent, even if the likelihood seems remote. Long-term care insurance can help cover expenses related to nursing homes or in-home care, which can quickly escalate.

Evaluate your risk tolerance and financial capabilities before deciding on a long-term care insurance policy. Understand the coverage details, potential costs, and limitations of each policy before committing. You might also consider alternative options, such as reverse mortgages or other financial strategies, if long-term care insurance costs are prohibitive.

Beyond the complexities of formal insurance plans, proactive healthcare management can considerably reduce expenses. Regular checkups and preventive care can help prevent costly illnesses in the long run. A healthy lifestyle, encompassing regular exercise and a balanced diet, can further reduce healthcare costs. Consider working with a healthcare cost management firm, should this prove beneficial in the long run, given the possibility of increased needs as time goes on. Remember, proactive healthcare management is as vital as having adequate insurance coverage.

Healthcare costs are a significant, often unpredictable, element of retirement planning. Prioritizing proactive healthcare management and seeking professional guidance in selecting appropriate supplemental insurance coverage are imperative to securing a financially sound and healthy retirement. While comprehensive planning may seem daunting, the peace of mind it provides far outweighs the effort invested. Remember, the goal isn't merely to survive financially in retirement but to thrive. A comprehensive healthcare plan is a crucial component of that ambition.

6.3 Long-Term Care

Long-term care is a significant, often overlooked, financial consideration for retirement. It's not just about nursing homes; it encompasses a wide spectrum of services designed to assist individuals with chronic illnesses, disabilities, or age-related decline in their ability to perform daily activities. These services can range from in-home assistance with bathing and dressing to more intensive care in assisted living facilities or skilled nursing facilities. The costs associated with these services can be substantial, quickly depleting retirement savings if not properly planned for.

Ignoring this aspect of retirement planning is a serious mistake. Many people assume Medicare will cover all healthcare costs, but this isn't true. Medicare primarily covers acute care, hospital stays, and some rehabilitation. Long-term care, however, is typically not covered extensively, leaving individuals responsible for a significant portion of the expenses. Failing to anticipate these costs can lead to financial hardship, forcing individuals to deplete retirement savings, sell assets, or even rely on family members for support—scenarios that could significantly impact their quality of life in their later years.

One of the most effective ways to mitigate the financial burden of long-term care is through insurance. Long-term care insurance policies provide coverage for a variety of services, including in-home care, assisted living, and nursing home care. These policies are designed to protect your assets and provide financial security should you require long-term care in the future. However, it's crucial to understand that long-term care insurance is not a one-size-fits-all solution. Policies vary significantly in terms of coverage, benefits, and cost, making it essential to carefully research and compare options. Selecting a policy that aligns with your individual needs and financial capabilities is paramount. The sooner you purchase a policy, the lower the premiums are likely to be, as your health is likely to be better.

Beyond insurance, exploring other financial strategies can help lessen the long-term care burden. These strategies often intertwine with other aspects of your retirement plan. For instance, maintaining a healthy investment portfolio is crucial to having the funds to cover long-term care expenses, whether or not you've invested in insurance. The accumulation of assets through diversified investments, as outlined in previous chapters, becomes an important cornerstone of preparedness. This ensures that you have a sufficient financial safety net for unforeseen circumstances. This includes actively managing your investments according to your risk tolerance and financial goals.

Proper estate planning also plays a vital role. Careful planning allows you to protect your assets and determine how they will be used to cover long-term care expenses or transferred to beneficiaries. This includes creating a comprehensive will and possibly establishing a trust to safeguard your assets. Such proactive planning can minimize the tax implications for your heirs, ensuring the smooth transfer of your estate while minimizing your family's financial burden. Legal and financial counsel is frequently needed here to navigate this complex area.

In addition to insurance and estate planning, exploring government programs and assistance options can alleviate some financial stress. Medicaid, a joint state and federal program, can help cover long-term care costs for those who meet certain income and asset requirements. Understanding the eligibility criteria and the application process for Medicaid is essential. Furthermore, veterans may be eligible for specific long-term care benefits through the Department of Veterans Affairs.

Finally, remember that planning for long-term care is not a one-time event; it's an ongoing process. Your needs and circumstances might change over time, requiring adjustments to your plan. Regularly reviewing your insurance policy, investment portfolio, and estate plan is crucial to ensuring that your plan remains appropriate as you age. This proactive approach allows you to make necessary changes and adapt to unforeseen circumstances. This commitment to ongoing planning is fundamental to securing your financial well-being during your retirement. Staying informed, seeking professional advice, and actively managing your long-term care plan will provide significant peace of mind, knowing that your future is financially secure.

6.4 Healthcare Savings

Healthcare costs represent a significant, often underestimated, portion of retirement expenses. Failing to adequately plan for these costs can severely impact your retirement lifestyle, potentially leading to financial hardship. Therefore, proactive strategies are crucial to mitigate these risks and secure your financial well-being. Understanding your options and implementing them early is key to successful retirement planning.

A cornerstone of healthcare planning in retirement is a thorough understanding of Medicare. While Medicare provides essential coverage, it doesn't cover everything. Knowing the nuances of Part A (hospital insurance), Part B (medical insurance), Part D (prescription drug insurance), and the supplemental options (Medigap) is essential. Consider carefully what gaps in coverage you might have and explore how Medigap plans can fill those gaps, preventing unexpected out-of-pocket expenses. Careful research and comparison shopping are necessary to select the plan best suited to your individual needs and budget. Consult with a qualified insurance agent to help navigate the complexities of Medicare and supplemental options. Ignoring this critical aspect could result in significant financial strain later in your retirement years.

Beyond Medicare, supplemental health insurance plays a critical role in managing healthcare costs. These plans, often offered by private insurers, can help cover expenses not reimbursed by Medicare, such as co-payments, deductibles, and certain services not covered by the basic Medicare plan. The cost of supplemental plans varies widely based on coverage levels and your health status. Before enrolling in a supplemental plan, carefully review the policy details, paying close attention to covered services, exclusions, and premiums. This careful review will ensure you're getting the best value for your investment, avoiding unnecessary expenses that can drain your retirement savings.

Long-term care insurance deserves serious consideration, as it can provide financial protection against the high costs associated with nursing homes or in-home care. The expenses related to long-term care can quickly deplete even substantial retirement savings. Long-term care insurance policies can help offset these substantial costs, protecting your assets and ensuring you receive the necessary care without financial strain. However, the cost of long-term care insurance itself can be significant, requiring careful consideration of the policy's terms, benefits, and the potential for future premium increases. Prescription drug costs are another significant factor impacting healthcare expenditures in retirement. Understanding Part D of Medicare and its coverage limitations is crucial. Investigate options like mail-order pharmacies or drug discount cards to help reduce costs. In addition, maintaining good health through preventative care can potentially reduce the overall need for prescription medications over time, indirectly reducing this aspect of your healthcare budget. Remember, preventative care is usually much cheaper than addressing problems later. This proactive approach demonstrates responsible fiscal planning and is very much needed for long term stability.

Health Savings Accounts (HSAs) are a powerful tool for those eligible to contribute. HSAs offer a tax-advantaged way to save for healthcare expenses. Contributions are tax deductible, grow tax-free, and withdrawals for qualified medical expenses are tax-free. For individuals with high-deductible health plans, an HSA can be an incredibly effective tool for managing healthcare costs. Careful planning and consistent contributions to an HSA can accumulate a substantial amount of money that will be there when you need it most. This tool, though not always accessible, can be a powerful financial asset for retirement security.

Finally, maintaining a healthy lifestyle through diet, exercise, and regular checkups can significantly contribute to lower healthcare costs over the long term. Prevention is always cheaper than cure. By proactively managing your health, you reduce your risk of developing serious health conditions requiring expensive treatment. This proactive strategy benefits not just your physical well-being but also your financial security in retirement. Prioritizing your health early can help you avoid significant medical expenses later in life, maximizing the value of your retirement savings. Remember that investing in your health is investing in your future financial security.

6.5 Prescription Costs

Prescription drug costs can significantly impact your retirement budget. Many retirees rely on multiple medications daily, and the expense can be staggering, especially without adequate insurance coverage. Understanding the landscape of prescription drug options and strategies for cost reduction is crucial for maintaining financial stability during your golden years. Negotiating prices with pharmacies, exploring generic alternatives, and taking advantage of prescription drug discount cards can help control these expenses.

Medicare Part D, the prescription drug coverage offered under Medicare, has its complexities. Knowing the different plan types—like Medicare Advantage plans with integrated prescription drug coverage or standalone Part D plans—is essential to finding the right fit for your needs and budget. Understanding your formulary, the list of covered drugs and their associated tiers, is also key. Higher tiers usually mean higher out-of-pocket costs. Carefully comparing plans annually during Medicare's open enrollment period is vital, as plan details and costs can change.

Don't overlook the potential for assistance programs. Many pharmaceutical companies offer patient assistance programs that provide free or discounted medications to eligible individuals. Additionally, various state and local programs exist to help low-income seniors access affordable prescription drugs. Researching these options and determining your eligibility is time well spent. You might find significant savings you weren't aware of. Remember to check the requirements for each program carefully.

Consider mail-order pharmacies. Often, ordering prescriptions through the mail can lead to substantial savings compared to local pharmacies. Many Part D plans offer mail-order options as part of their benefit structure, frequently at lower costs than filling individual prescriptions at retail locations. This is especially beneficial for individuals taking multiple medications regularly. It's convenient and can often lead to considerable cost savings.

Regularly review your medication list with your physician. Are all your medications necessary? Are there newer, more cost-effective alternatives? A proactive conversation with your doctor can lead to adjustments that not only reduce costs but also potentially improve your overall health. This proactive approach will help you make informed choices about your prescriptions, leading to more manageable and affordable healthcare costs in retirement.

Beyond these strategies, carefully tracking your prescription expenses is paramount. Maintain records of your prescriptions, costs, and reimbursements. This meticulous record-keeping helps you monitor your spending and identify potential areas for savings. It also proves invaluable during any insurance claim disputes or discussions with your healthcare providers. Accurate tracking is the bedrock of responsible healthcare budgeting.

The financial burden of prescription drugs is a significant concern for many retirees, but with careful planning and strategic utilization of available resources, it can become more manageable. Proactive engagement with your healthcare team, understanding your insurance coverage, and exploring cost-saving options can alleviate the stress of this substantial expense. Remember, planning for prescription costs is as crucial to a secure retirement as planning for other essential expenses. The key is to be informed, prepared and persistent in finding the most cost-effective solutions for your individual circumstances. Don't hesitate to ask questions and seek professional guidance; it's a worthwhile investment in your retirement well-being. Your health and financial security are deeply interconnected during retirement; careful attention to both is crucial for a comfortable and fulfilling later life.

7 Chapter 7: Enjoying Retirement

Creating a realistic budget is paramount. This isn't about deprivation; it's about mindful spending. Start by meticulously tracking your current expenses, categorizing them into necessities (housing, utilities, food), discretionary spending (travel, hobbies), and healthcare costs. Compare these figures against your projected retirement income, revealing any potential shortfalls. This initial analysis forms the bedrock of your retirement budget. Remember, flexibility is key; unforeseen expenses always arise, so include a contingency fund. Consider exploring part-time employment opportunities, not solely for extra income but also to maintain social interaction and a sense of purpose. Many retirees find fulfilling part-time work enriches their lives significantly beyond financial benefits. Don't underestimate the power of downsizing. A smaller home can reduce property taxes, maintenance costs, and energy bills, freeing up funds for leisure activities. This isn't about sacrificing comfort; it's about aligning your living space with your needs and lifestyle in this new chapter.

Maintaining a healthy lifestyle is inextricably linked to enjoying a fulfilling retirement. Regular exercise isn't just about physical well-being; it boosts mental acuity and reduces healthcare expenses in the long run. Social engagement is crucial; loneliness can impact your well-being significantly, so actively seek opportunities for interaction. Join clubs, volunteer, or reconnect with old friends. These activities provide emotional sustenance, combatting isolation and enriching your daily life. Explore new hobbies; learning something new keeps your mind engaged and expands your horizons. Whether it's painting, gardening, or learning a new language, the pursuit of knowledge and personal growth is profoundly rewarding. Consider travel, but plan wisely. Budget-friendly options exist; explore off-season travel, consider domestic destinations, or opt for more affordable accommodations. The point isn't to travel lavishly but to experience new cultures and environments, broadening your perspectives.

Financial freedom in retirement doesn't necessitate extravagant spending. Instead, it's about achieving a balance between financial security and enjoying life's experiences. Prioritize experiences over material possessions; invest in enriching activities that add value to your life rather than accumulating unnecessary items. This shift in perspective will enhance your overall satisfaction and well-being. Engage in activities that challenge your mind; this can be anything from pursuing intellectual interests such as reading and learning to participating in activities that require problem-solving skills such as puzzles or games. Mental stimulation is vital for maintaining cognitive sharpness and overall well-being throughout retirement. Don't forget the importance of giving back to your community. Volunteering not only offers a sense of purpose but also fosters social connections and contributes positively to society. The sense of fulfillment derived from helping others is invaluable and can significantly enhance your sense of well-being. Retirement is not an ending; it's a new beginning, a time for pursuing passions and enjoying life to the fullest.

Retirement offers a unique opportunity to reinvent oneself. Embrace this newfound flexibility; use it to pursue long-dormant hobbies, learn new skills, or explore different aspects of your personality. Don't be afraid to step outside your comfort zone and experiment with new things. It's a chance to discover hidden talents and passions. Building and maintaining strong relationships with family and friends is crucial. Regular social interaction provides emotional support and combats loneliness, two common challenges for retirees. Schedule regular time for these important connections, whether it is a weekly family dinner or a monthly get-together with friends. Strong social bonds enhance overall well-being and contribute significantly to enjoying your retirement years. Remember, retirement isn't solely about financial planning; it's about creating a fulfilling lifestyle. By integrating these strategies into your retirement plan, you can create a balance between financial security and personal satisfaction, making your retirement a truly rewarding and enjoyable experience. This new chapter of your life is a chance to celebrate your achievements, pursue personal passions, and create lasting memories. It's a well-deserved reward for your years of hard work and planning.

7.1 Budgeting in Retirement

Creating a realistic budget is paramount to enjoying a comfortable retirement. It's not about deprivation; it's about mindful spending aligned with your revised income stream. Start by meticulously listing all your anticipated expenses – housing, utilities, groceries, transportation, healthcare, entertainment, and travel. Don't underestimate the costs; factor in potential inflation and unexpected expenses. This detailed list will form the foundation of your retirement budget.

Next, honestly assess your income sources. This includes Social Security, pensions, retirement account withdrawals, and any other income streams you anticipate. Be realistic; don't overestimate your potential earnings, particularly from investments, whose returns can be volatile. Consider worst-case scenarios and plan accordingly. It's crucial to maintain a buffer for unforeseen circumstances.

Now, compare your estimated expenses to your projected income. If your expenses exceed your income, you'll need to make adjustments. This isn't a time for panic, but rather for thoughtful recalibration. You might explore downsizing your home, reducing unnecessary expenses, or finding ways to supplement your income through part-time work or consulting. Consider your priorities; what truly matters to you in retirement? This will help you prioritize where to allocate your resources.

Remember, your budget isn't set in stone. It should be a living document, regularly reviewed and adjusted as circumstances change. Review your budget at least quarterly or annually. This allows you to track your spending, identify areas for improvement, and make any necessary adjustments to keep your finances in line with your goals. Life throws curveballs; having a flexible budget allows you to navigate unexpected expenses without jeopardizing your financial stability.

Unexpected healthcare costs often derail retirement budgets. Medicare covers a significant portion of healthcare expenses, but it doesn't cover everything. Supplementing your coverage with a Medigap plan or a Medicare Advantage plan can protect you from substantial out-of-pocket expenses. Plan for potential long-term care needs; these costs can be astronomical. Investigate long-term care insurance or explore other options to mitigate the financial burden of potential long-term care. Proactive planning will safeguard your financial well-being.

Beyond healthcare, consider unexpected home repairs. Older homes require more maintenance, and these repairs can be costly. Create a contingency fund specifically for home maintenance. Regularly set aside a portion of your income for this purpose; this will prevent unexpected repair costs from creating a financial strain. This proactive approach will provide peace of mind and ensure that your retirement funds remain secure.

Finally, remember that retirement is a new chapter in your life, not an end. It's a time to pursue passions, travel, and spend time with loved ones. Your budget should reflect this. While saving and responsible spending are crucial, don't deprive yourself of the things that bring you joy. A well-structured budget allows for both financial security and fulfillment in retirement. Your retirement budget should support your lifestyle choices; it's not simply about restricting spending but about aligning your expenses with your values and aspirations for this new phase of life. This balance ensures both financial security and enjoyment of your retirement years.

7.2 Lifestyle Adjustments

Downsizing your home might seem daunting, but consider the benefits. A smaller home means lower property taxes, reduced maintenance costs, and potentially less energy consumption - all contributing significantly to your retirement budget. Think about it: less cleaning, less yard work, less overall upkeep. That frees up your time and energy for the activities you truly enjoy. Perhaps a cozy cottage near the ocean, or a vibrant condo in a bustling city center—the possibilities open up when you release yourself from the constraints of a large, possibly outdated, family home. The financial advantages are substantial and directly impact your long-term financial security, allowing for more leisure travel or pursuing long-held hobbies. It's about finding a space that perfectly reflects your changed circumstances and priorities, a space that adds to the enjoyment of your retirement rather than taking from it. The emotional adjustment is worth the peace of mind that financial stability brings.

Rethinking your transportation is another key area. Are you really needing that extra vehicle? For many retirees, one reliable car is more than sufficient, especially if they live near amenities or plan to utilize public transportation. Selling an extra car eliminates insurance premiums, maintenance costs, and the ongoing expense of fuel. These savings add up quickly, potentially freeing up funds for travel, hobbies, or investments. You'll be surprised by how much money you could save. Consider the environmental benefits too; reducing your carbon footprint contributes to a sustainable lifestyle and, perhaps, a clearer conscience. This simple shift can lead to significant long-term financial savings and a greater sense of environmental responsibility. Plus, the reduced stress of car ownership can improve your overall wellbeing.

Social connections are invaluable during retirement. Maintain active engagement with your community. Consider volunteering your time; many organizations welcome the skills and experience retirees offer. This not only provides a sense of purpose but also opens doors to new friendships and social networks. Volunteering offers mental stimulation, prevents isolation, and connects you with like-minded individuals. Your skills and life experiences become invaluable assets, making a positive impact on your community while benefiting your personal wellbeing immensely. Remember, retirement isn't about ending; it's about transitioning to a new chapter, filled with purpose and rewarding relationships. Engaging actively in your community is a win-win situation; you give back and receive so much in return.

Re-evaluating your leisure activities can make a substantial difference. Perhaps you've always dreamed of learning Italian, taking up painting, or joining a hiking club. Retirement offers the ideal time to pursue these passions. These new interests can enhance your quality of life while often being more cost-effective than previous leisure pursuits. Think outside the box; exploring local parks, attending free community events, or joining a book club can provide enriching experiences without breaking the bank. The satisfaction derived from these activities outweighs the financial aspect, contributing to a more fulfilling and less expensive retirement. Remember, personal enrichment is crucial for a successful retirement, and often the most enriching things are surprisingly inexpensive.

Dining habits play a crucial role in managing your retirement budget. While indulging occasionally is acceptable, reducing restaurant meals can result in significant savings. Cooking at home more often not only saves money but also encourages healthier eating. Consider meal prepping for the week ahead, reducing food waste, and taking advantage of seasonal produce. It's not about deprivation; it's about mindful consumption. You can still enjoy occasional outings, but making home-cooked meals your mainstay can significantly reduce your monthly food expenses. It's a shift that not only benefits your wallet but also your health and well-being. A proactive and thoughtful approach to food can enhance both your physical and financial health.

Finally, consider your entertainment habits. Streaming services, while convenient, can accumulate considerable costs over time. Evaluate your subscriptions; perhaps you could share accounts with family or friends or choose a more budget-friendly option. Remember, libraries offer an extensive collection of books, movies, and other media at no cost. Exploring free community events, attending concerts in the park, or joining a local theater group can provide just as much, if not more, enjoyment, at a considerably lower price point. The key is to find affordable and enjoyable ways to remain entertained, enriching your retirement years without straining your budget. Finding inexpensive, alternative options for entertainment allows you to maintain a fulfilling and stimulating social life whilst being financially prudent. This conscientious approach will maintain a healthy financial outlook whilst allowing you to live a happy and carefree retirement.

www.ingramcontent.com/pod-product-compliance
Lightning Source LLC
LaVergne TN
LVHW022018200926
848481LV00007B/2452
* 9 7 9 8 3 4 8 5 9 6 0 4 0 *